# TOP CARS

# JAGUAR

**Lee Stacy**

**W**
**FRANKLIN WATTS**
LONDON • SYDNEY

First published in 2005 by
Franklin Watts
96 Leonard Street
London EC2A 4XD

Franklin Watts Australia
45–51 Huntley Street
Alexandria
NSW 2015

ISBN 0 7496 6007 4

A CIP catalogue record for this book is available
from the British Library

Printed in China

**For The Brown Reference Group plc**
Editor: Bridget Giles
Managing Editor: Tim Cooke
Design Manager: Lynne Ross
Children's Publisher: Anne O'Daly
Production Director: Alastair Gourlay
Editorial Director: Lindsey Lowe

**Credits**
Pictures: IMP AB
Text: The Brown Reference Group plc/
IMP AB

**Note to parents and teachers**
Every effort has been made by the Publishers to ensure that
the websites in this book are suitable for children,
that they are of the highest educational value,
and that they contain no inappropriate or
offensive material. However, because of the
nature of the Internet, it is impossible to
guarantee that the contents of these sites will
not be altered. We strongly advise that Internet
access is supervised by a responsible adult.

Some words are shown in **bold**, like this.

You can find out what they mean by looking

at the bottom right of most right-hand pages.

You can also find most of the words in the

Glossary on page 30.

# Contents

# Introduction

The British car manufacturer Jaguar was started by William Lyons (1901–1985). In 1922 he set up a company that made sidecars for motorcycles. By the late 1940s the company also made cars and was named Jaguar Cars Limited. At first Jaguar made mostly sports cars. By the 1960s the company was also famous for saloons and race cars. William Lyons retired in 1972, and for several years the company did not

Jaguar's logo is the head of the big cat of the same name, which is famous for speed and power.

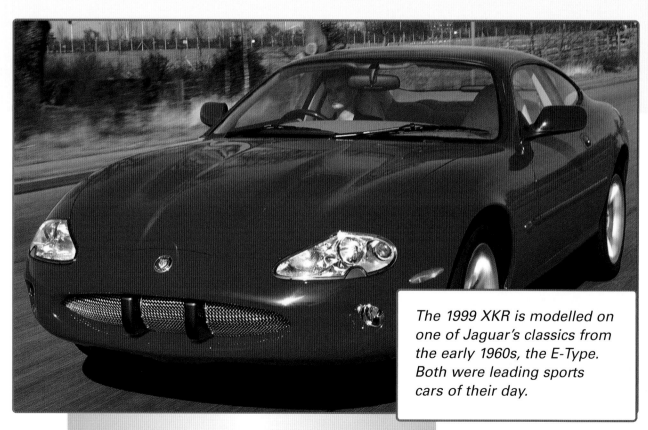

The 1999 XKR is modelled on one of Jaguar's classics from the early 1960s, the E-Type. Both were leading sports cars of their day.

do so well, even though it produced some classic cars. In 1990 Jaguar was bought by the U.S. car giant Ford. Ford's resources and Jaguar's experience of making luxury cars combined to produce some modern classics to add to Jaguar's roster. Some of the company's outstanding models are the E-Type, XJ12 HE, XKR, S-Type, limited-edition XJ220 and the XJR.

*Jaguar's XJ220 is one of the fastest sports cars in the world. It is also one of the rarest. Only a few were made in the early 1990s. Each vehicle was assembled completely by hand.*

*The XJR is one of Jaguar's most popular saloons. It mixes power with style. The engine is a supercharged V8. The interior has both leather upholstery and high-tech gadgets.*

# Jaguar E-Type

**W**hen Jaguar introduced the E-Type in 1961, the public had never seen anything like it before. Critics said that it looked like something from outer space or out of a science-fiction film. Most people agreed that it was sleek and beautiful, however, and performed outstandingly. When production of the E-Type ended in 1975, more than 72,000 had been built. Today the E-Type is considered one of the great sports cars of all time.

## Milestones

### 1961
Jaguar introduces the E-Type at the Geneva Motor Show. The sports car is so popular that Jaguar receives many advance orders from buyers.

### 1968
The Series II E-Types are given larger bonnets and bigger front and rear lights.

### 1971
The Series III models are launched. Among them is the Roadster with a V12 engine.

### 1975
Jaguar ends production of the E-Type.

**Vital Statistics for the 1961 E-Type Roadster**

| | |
|---|---|
| Top speed: | *241 km/h (150 mph)* |
| 0–60 mph: | *7.3 seconds* |
| Engine: | *In-line six* |
| Engine size: | *3,781 cc (230.7 ci)* |
| Power: | *265 bhp at 5,500 rpm* |
| Weight: | *1,117 kg (2,463 lb)* |
| Fuel economy: | *14.5 mpg* |

The *fascia* in the E-Type is simple but stylish. It is also functional, with all the gauges needed for a sports car.

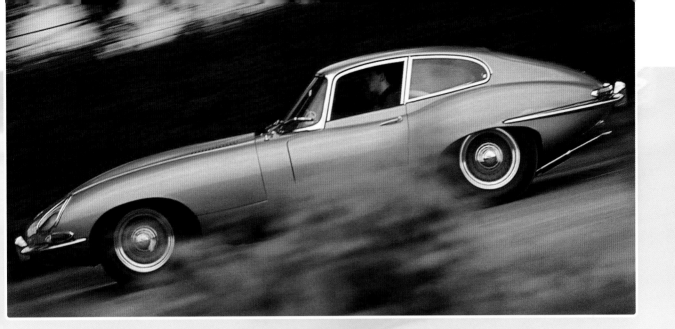

*"The E-Type is a joy to drive. The view down the never-ending bonnet promises the thrill of a lifetime, and that's just what the E-Type delivers."*

Jaguar produced a lightweight E-Type in 1963. The body was aluminium, and the engine was made of **alloy**. Both innovations helped to lessen the overall weight of the car.

| | |
|---|---|
| **Alloy** | A generally strong but lightweight metal made by mixing other metals. |
| **Fascia** | A panel inside the car that holds instruments displaying information for the driver. |

# Specifications

*Most of the credit for the classic look and outstanding performance of the E-Type belongs to Malcolm Sayer and William Lyons. Sayer specialized in **aerodynamics**, and Lyons, the head of Jaguar, was one of the best car designers in Britain.*

**Fold-away soft top**

*The soft top on the E-Type convertible folds neatly away in a space behind the seats.*

The E-Type might look long, but its wheelbase—the length from the front axle to the back axle—is shorter than on most other Jaguar sports cars of the time.

Most sports cars in the early 1960s had bodies that were supported on a horizontal frame called a chassis. On the E-Type, the body itself, not the chassis, supports the car.

**Aerodynamic headlights**

*Early headlights were covered in hard, clear plastic to make the car more aerodynamic.*

**Front-hinged bonnet**

*The E-Type's engine is very long. To gain access to it, the bonnet is hinged at the front of the car, near the nose.*

**Heat vents**

*The engine produces a lot of heat. The bonnet has 14 rows of vents to let the heat escape.*

**Rear suspension**

*The E-Type was Jaguar's first model to have independent rear suspension to give a smoother ride.*

| | |
|---|---|
| **Aerodynamics** | Designing objects that pass smoothly through the air. |
| **Suspension** | A system that supports a car and makes it travel more smoothly. |
| **Vents** | Openings that allow exhaust fumes to escape. |

# Jaguar XJ12 HE

The XJ12 was one of Jaguar's most successful luxury **saloons** of the 1970s. The car used a lot of fuel, however, at a time when petrol was becoming more expensive. In 1979 Jaguar came up with a solution: the XJ12 HE. 'HE' stands for High Efficiency. The new model performed just as well as the old XJ12 but travelled farther on the same amount of fuel. From 1979 to 1993, when production ended, only a few minor changes were made to the XJ12 HE.

## Vital Statistics for the 1985 Jaguar XJ12 HE

| | |
|---|---|
| Top speed: | *241 km/h (150 mph)* |
| 0–60 mph: | *8.1 seconds* |
| Engine: | *V12* |
| Engine size: | *5,345 cc (326.2 ci)* |
| Power: | *299 bhp at 5,500 rpm* |
| Weight: | *1,922 kg (4,237 lb)* |
| Fuel economy: | *18 mpg* |

*The cockpit in the XJ12 HE is spacious and comfortable. Wooden inlay on the fascia is a traditional feature of Jaguar cars.*

## *Milestones*

**1972**

Jaguar begins production of the XJ12 saloon.

**1979**

One of the new models in the Series III XJ range is the XJ12 HE. It comes with a V12 engine adapted from the one used in the Series III E-type.

**1981**

After several improvements, the fuel efficiency of the XJ12 HE increases from 13 to 16 mpg.

**1993**

Jaguar decides to end production of the XJ12 HE.

*"The change to the new HE cylinder heads made no difference to the extremely smooth and quiet V12, which is matched by incredible refinement throughout."*

*In 1960 Jaguar bought the German car maker Daimler. In the early 1980s Jaguar used the XJ12 body on its own Daimler Double Six model. The only exterior difference between the cars was a new radiator grille.*

**Saloon**     A car with two or four doors and seats for four or more people.

# Specifications

The exterior of the XJ12 HE is based on the XJ6, an earlier Jaguar classic. The interior is stylish, in keeping with Jaguar's high standards. Under the bonnet, the engine is a modified V12. Head to head, the XJ12 HE outperformed its competition.

**Efficient radiator**

To help cool the large V12 engine, Jaguar separated the radiator into a top half and a bottom half. This horizontally divided radiator cools the engine more efficiently.

**V12 engine**

In the early 1980s, the XJ12 HE's V12 engine was top class. Having two valves per cylinder, the engine created 299 bhp at 5,500 rpm.

In the first XJ12, the transmission was a poor automatic one that owners complained about. Jaguar's solution was to adapt a much better General Motors transmission for the car.

Another difference between the original XJ12 and the XJ12 HE is the size of the front bumper. The improved model came with a larger bumper that gave more protection.

**For turning corners**

To add extra control for turning corners, a limited-slip **differential** has been installed.

### Lightweight alloy wheels

*One of the differences between the original XJ12 and the XJ12 HE is the wheels. The first model had steel disc-type wheels. To lighten the weight of the car and to make it more fuel efficient, the XJ12 HE has alloy wheels.*

### Roomy boot

*Even for a saloon, the boot is exceptionally spacious. There is plenty of room for the largest luggage.*

**Axle**  A shaft that runs across the width of the car and on which two wheels are attached. A car has two axles, one in the front and one in the rear.

**Differential**  Gears that make the wheels on either side of an **axle** spin at either the same rate or, for instance, when turning a corner, at different rates to maintain balance and speed.

# Jaguar XKR

**T**echnically, the XKR is one of Jaguar's most advanced cars. It was one of several 1990s models that benefited from research funded by Jaguar's new owners, the Ford Motor Company. In looks, the XKR resembles Jaguar's older models, such as the E-Type of the early 1960s. Introduced in 1998, the XKR is available as either a **coupé** or a **convertible**. Both versions perform well, but the convertible is slightly less stable because it does not have a hard top.

### Vital Statistics for the 1999 Jaguar XKR

| | |
|---|---|
| Top speed: | *249 km/h (155 mph)* |
| 0–60 mph: | *5.1 seconds* |
| Engine: | *V8* |
| Engine size: | *3,996 cc (243.9 ci)* |
| Power: | *370 bhp at 6,150 rpm* |
| Weight: | *1,746 kg (3,850 lb)* |
| Fuel economy: | *14 mpg* |

## Milestones

### 1996

Jaguar, now owned by Ford, introduces the XKR at the Geneva Motor Show. It is a critical success.

### 1997

The XJR is introduced *(see page 26)*. It has a new type of V8 engine. Jaguar, with Ford's help, plans to adapt the XJR's V8 engine for the coupé and convertible XKR.

### 1998

As promised, Jaguar's new V8 engine is included in the latest version of the XKR, along with other changes.

*Jaguar included the latest gadgets and styling in the two-door XKR. The cockpit is one of the roomiest of any coupé or convertible.*

"*Combining outstanding handling prowess with a soft, supple ride is not easy, but Jaguar has done a remarkable job. It is a refined cruiser of the highest order.*"

The XKR soft-top convertible is more expensive than the hardtop version, yet critics claim that the ride in the hardtop is smoother and the car easier to control. Despite this, the soft-top XKR is very popular with drivers.

**Convertible**   A type of car that has a top that can be lowered or removed.

**Coupé**   A two-door car that usually seats four people.

# Specifications

The XKR is just one of Jaguar's models to have the supercharged V8 engine. The extra power suits the convertible, making it perform the way a sports car should. To cope with the engine's power, the car has a Mercedes-Benz **transmission**.

**Supercharged engine**

The all-alloy V8 engine has 32 valves. The pistons in the eight cylinders are modified to move more smoothly and to increase engine power.

**Front**

Like the 1960s E-Type, the XKR has an aerodynamic nose and front-hinged bonnet.

To solve the problem of frost building on the rear window of the soft top, Jaguar offers a removable glass rear window that is electrically heated.

The power and speed are so great on the XKR that the car uses special disc brakes. The brakes are 30 cm (12 inches) in diameter. They are vented to release heat and have pads for the high friction created when in use.

**Large rear wheels**

The rear wheels are 46 cm (18 inches) in diameter, which is large for this size car. Big wheels are needed in the rear because the XKR has huge vented **disc brakes**.

### Power soft top

It only takes 20 seconds for the electrically operated soft top to fold away.

### Windscreen frame

To support the large windscreen, the model has a reinforced frame. The frame is also designed to protect the driver if the car rolls over.

**Disc brakes**     A brake with a rotating disc inside the wheel mechanism. A clip pinches the disc to stop the wheel spinning.

**Transmission**     The speed-changing gears and other parts that transmit power from engine to wheels.

# Jaguar S-Type

The first S-Type was produced from 1963 to 1968. Jaguar brought back the range in 1998, using a combination of Jaguar and Ford parts. The body and interior are Jaguar, but the **chassis** is borrowed from Ford's Lincoln LS. Saloons are generally larger in the United States of America than in Europe, so the Lincoln chassis makes the S-Type bigger than its European rivals. Its wheelbase (distance between front and back axles) is one of the longest on any Jaguar.

## Milestones

**1963**

The carmaker released the S-Type, a revised, second Jaguar in the range of cars to include a saloon. The S-Type

**1968**

The S-Type is replaced by the XJ model.

**1996**

At the Birmingham Motor Show, Jaguar revives the S-Type. Its identity is that of a Lincoln model.

**1999**

The S-Type V8 is available around the world, normally some parts are new.

| Vital Statistics for the 1999 Jaguar S-Type 4.0 V8 | |
| --- | --- |
| Top speed: | 241 km/h (150 mph) |
| 0–60 mph: | 6.6 seconds |
| Engine: | V8 |
| Engine size: | 3,996 cc (243.9 ci) |
| Power: | 281 bhp at 6,100 rpm |
| Weight: | 1,710 kg (3,770 lb) |
| Fuel economy: | 23 mpg |

Although the S-Type interior maintains Jaguar's superior standards, some critics argue that it has lost its sleekness and looks more like the inside of a Ford Lincoln.

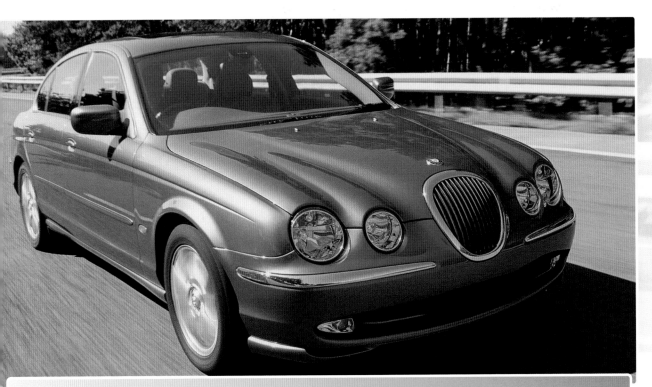

*"Jaguar's idea to make a true driver's car succeeded.*
*In all respects, this is a Jaguar through and through."*

Jaguar offers a choice of either a V6 or V8 engine for the S-Type. The V6 is the economical choice, giving owners better fuel efficiency. The V8 is the more expensive and more powerful option. At top speed, the S-Type with the V8 engine can reach 241 km/h (150 mph).

**Chassis**     The supporting frame of the car onto which the body is fixed.

# Specifications

According to some critics, the revived S-Type is one of the most important cars Jaguar has ever made. One thing that makes it so popular is the way it handles. From front to rear, it is perfectly balanced. It was also highly advanced technically when launched.

**Electric sun roof**

The electrically controlled glass sun roof is one of many modern options on the S-Type.

**Engine choice**

The S-Type has either a V6 or V8 engine. The V6 was made in the USA, and the V8 is adapted from Jaguar's XJ8 and XK8 models. Both engines give enormous power for their sizes.

The transmission in the V6 is only available as a five-speed automatic in the United States of America. Outside the USA, a manual transmission is optional.

As with many modern cars, the S-Type is fitted with rear sensors that give off a warning when the car is too close to another object. This helps to avoid bumps and scrapes.

**Lincoln suspension**

The S-Type is built on a Lincoln's **chassis** and suspension system. It is a double-wishbone suspension made mostly of aluminium.

### Perfect balance

*Jaguar spent many hours making sure the front and rear of the S-Type was evenly balanced. One result of this perfect balance is that the car takes corners easily and smoothly.*

### Deep boot

*Because the S-Type has an American chassis, it also has a wide and deep boot. There is plenty of storage for large luggage.*

**Chassis**    The supporting frame on which a car's body is fixed.

# Jaguar XJ220

The Jaguar XJ220 is one of the most unusual cars ever built. The car was designed and built by staff at Jaguar in their spare time and without pay. It was a product of love, not a business decision. The Jaguar engineers built it to prove that they could make the fastest sports car in the world. The XJ220 was in production for just two years, and only 281 were built. It cost around £400,000, so few could afford the car. One belongs to the singer Elton John.

## Milestones

**1988**

Decision in October, that the first working model of the XJ220 is shown to the public.

**1989**

The XJ220 is launched. It has a V6 turbo engine and five-speed manual transmission.

**1992**

At a track in Italy, the XJ220 is clocked at 349.4 km/h (217.1 mph), making it the fastest road car in the world.

**1994**

Production of the XJ220 ends. Only 281 built.

### Vital Statistics for the 1993 Jaguar XJ220

| | |
|---|---|
| Top speed: | 335 km/h (208 mph) |
| 0–60 mph: | 3.8 seconds |
| Engine: | V6 |
| Engine size: | 3,491 cc (231 ci) |
| Power: | 542 bhp at 7,200 rpm |
| Weight: | 1,470 kg (3,241 lb) |
| Fuel economy: | 12.9 mpg |

The fascia of the XJ220 included what were the most advanced gadgets and instrument panel available in the early 1990s.

"*The XJ220 is unique, cocooning you in traditional Jaguar luxury. But make no mistake, this Jaguar crouches low like a predator ready to pounce.*"

Three panels lift up on the XJ220. The front bonnet exposes the **radiator**. The glass lid behind the driver gives access to the engine. In the rear, the boot lid covers a small luggage area, just big enough for a couple of briefcases.

**Radiator** A part of the cooling system that stores liquid to cool the engine.

# Specifications

The XJ220 looks quick — and it is. The body is based on one of Jaguar's 1960s racing cars, the XJ13. The speed, more than 330 km/h (200 mph), comes from the latest in racing technology. The only competition is from Bugatti and Lamborghini cars.

**Posh interior**

The **cockpit** includes leather seats, thick carpets and a top-of-the-range sound system.

**Lightweight body**

The body is made entirely of lightweight aluminium. The chassis is also aluminium. It is bonded to the body with adhesive since aluminium cannot be welded.

Each XJ220 was assembled by hand. This took a lot of time, but it is one of the things that helped to make the car special. Once finished, each car was painted one of only five colours: blue, grey, green, maroon or silver.

To help cool the engine there are two sets of vents. Behind the doors, large oval-shaped vents take in air that cools the radiators. On the bonnet, long curved vents let hot air escape from the engine compartment.

**No spare**

There is no spare tyre. If one goes flat, it can be inflated with an aerosol spray that also temporarily seals the puncture. The tyre can then be driven for up to 97 km (60 miles) at a top speed of 49 km/h (30 mph).

### Display glass for engine

The lid covering the engine is glass in order to show off the most important feature of the XJ220.

### Hidden headlights

The headlights are lowered into the nose when not in use. This helps the car's aerodynamics.

**Cockpit**     The part of the car where the driver sits.

# Jaguar XJR

The XJR is one of the fastest saloons available because of its supercharged V8 engine. Jaguar's superior styling and attention to detail add to its attraction. Capable of a top speed of 249 km/h (155 mph), the XJR stands out among its competition, the Mercedes-Benz E55 AMG and the Cadillac STS. One reason for the XJR's power and top performance is that the car's engine and chassis have been adapted from Jaguar's XK8 sports car.

## Vital Statistics for the 1998 Jaguar XJR

| | |
|---|---|
| Top speed: | *249 km/h (155 mph)* |
| 0–60 mph: | *5.4 seconds* |
| Engine: | *V8* |
| Engine size: | *3,996 cc (243.9 ci)* |
| Power: | *370 bhp at 6,150 rpm* |
| Weight: | *1,848 kg (4,075 lb)* |
| Fuel economy: | *19 mpg* |

## Milestones

### 1994
The XJ saloon range is introduced with a powerful six-cylinder engine.

### 1996
Jaguar's XK8 sports car is the first with the supercharged V8 engine.

### 1997
The successful XJ saloon receives the supercharged V8 engine from the XK8. The more powerful saloon is named the XJR and can go from 0 to 97 km/h (60 mph) in only 5.4 seconds. The interior and body are also improved.

*High-tech options, such as a superior music system and fully adjustable seats, help make the experience of driving Jaguar's XJR an unrivalled pleasure.*

"*The only word to describe the seamless flow of power from the supercharged V8 engine is awesome. If you floor the* **accelerator** *there is instant acceleration on an epic scale.*"

Many critics believe that the XJR is one of the finest Jaguars ever made. This is due to its perfect combination of style and power. The supercharged V8 is technically one of the best Jaguar engines, while the interior is top-of-the-range Jaguar.

**Accelerator**   The foot pedal the driver uses to increase the speed of the car.

# Specifications

*Among top saloons, the XJR is near the front of the pack. Jaguar's skill plus Ford's research budget have created a fast and powerful car. The Computer Active Technology Suspension (CATS) ensures passengers get a smooth ride.*

### Powerful and innovative engine

The V8 engine in the XJR was adapted from the XK8 sports car. Its features include an aluminium quad-cam with a modified camshaft that varies the timing of taking fuel into the engine.

### Automatic headlights

The headlights have light sensors. When the light outside dims, the headlights switch on automatically.

### CATS suspension

To give the smoothest ride possible, the XJR is fitted with the Computer Active Technology Suspension system (CATS). Its suspension system has top-of-the-range **shock absorbers**.

The XJR's V8 engine produces far too much **torque** for any Jaguar transmission to cope with. To handle the high torque, a Mercedes-Benz S600 transmission is used.

The electronics are highly advanced. The onboard computer processes information rapidly and diagnoses any problem that the car develops.

### Large boot

The boot measures 0.41 cubic metres (14.5 cubic feet). It is large enough to take several big suitcases without the passengers even knowing the luggage is there.

### Luxury interior

As in all luxury Jaguars, the interior of the XJR is very comfortable, with leather seats and deep carpets. It is also full of electronic equipment and has a high-quality sound system.

| | |
|---|---|
| **Shock absorbers** | Spring-like devices that help to smooth a bumpy ride. |
| **Torque** | The force that causes an object to rotate. An engine creates torque to turn a crankshaft. |

# Glossary

**accelerator:** *The foot pedal the driver uses to increase the speed of the car.*

**aerodynamic:** *Designed to pass smoothly through the air.*

**axle:** *A shaft that runs across the width of the car and on which two wheels are attached. A car has two axles, one in the front and one in the rear.*

**chassis:** *The supporting frame of the car on which the body is fixed.*

**cockpit:** *The area where the driver sits.*

**convertible:** *A type of car with a top that can be lowered or removed.*

**coupé:** *A two-door car that usually seats four people.*

**fascia:** *A panel inside the car that holds instruments displaying information for the driver. Also, dashboard.*

**radiator:** *A part of the cooling system that stores liquid to cool the engine with.*

**saloon:** *A car with two or four doors that seats four or more people.*

**shock absorbers:** *Spring-like devices that help to smooth out a bumpy ride.*

**suspension:** *A system of springs that support a car and make it travel more smoothly.*

**transmission:** *Speed-changing gears and other parts that transmit power from engine to wheels.*

**vents:** *Openings that allow exhaust fumes to escape.*

## Further information

### websites

*www.cyberparent.com/wheels/jaguar.htm*
History of Jaguar

*http://auto.howstuffworks.com/engine.htm*
How Stuff Works: Car Engines

*www.jag-lovers.org*
Jag-lovers: A Jaguar enthusiasts' site

*www.jaguar.com*
Jaguar

### books

● Beck, Paul. **Uncover a Race Car: An Uncover It Book.** Silver Dolphin Books, 2003.

● Buckley, Martin. **Jaguar: Fifty Years of Speed and Style.** Motorbooks International, 2002.

● Sutton, Richard. **Eyewitness: Car.** Dorling Kindersley Publishing, 2000.

● Thorley, Nigel. **Jaguar: All the Cars.** Motorbooks International, 2003.

# Index